EDGE BOOKS

THE TECH BEHIND RACE CARS

by Steve Goldsworthy

CAPSTONE PRESS
a capstone imprint

Edge Books are published by Capstone Press,
1710 Roe Crest Drive, North Mankato, Minnesota 56003
www.capstonepub.com

Library of Congress Cataloging-in-Publication Data
Names: Goldsworthy, Steve, author.
Title: The tech behind race cars / by Steve Goldsworthy.
Description: First edition. | North Mankato, Minnesota: Capstone Press, [2020] | Series: Edge books. Tech on wheels. | Audience: Age 8-14. | Audience: Grades 7 to 8.
Identifiers: LCCN 2018060565l
ISBN 9781543574210 (hardcover) | ISBN 9781543574234 (ebook pdf)
Subjects: LCSH: Automobiles, Racing—Juvenile literature.
Classification: LCC TL236 .G643 2020 | DDC 629.228/5—dc23
LC record available at https://lccn.loc.gov/2018060565

Editorial Credits
Carrie Braulick Sheely, editor; Jennifer Bergstrom, designer; Eric Gohl, media researcher; Katy LaVigne, production specialist

Photo Credits
Alamy: Arco Images GmbH, 18, Richard McDowell, 8; Dreamstime: Walter Arce, 20, 25; Getty Images: RacingOne, 6; Newscom: Cover Images/Renault, 29, Icon Sportswire/Malcolm Hope, 13, NOTIMEX/Francisco Estrada, 26, Reuters/Arnd Wiegmann, 11, Reuters/Denis Balibouse, 28, USA Today Sports/Brian Spurlock, 4, ZUMA Press/Ben Birchall, 19; Shutterstock: Abdul Razak Latif, 21, action sports, 14, Action Sports Photography, 10, 23, David Acosta Allely, cover, Doug James, 16, ermess, 22, Ev. Safronov, 9, Nixx Photography, 12

Design Elements: Shutterstock

Printed in and bound in the USA.
PA70

TABLE OF CONTENTS

CHAPTER 1
The Need for Speed 4

CHAPTER 2
What Makes a Race Car Fast? 8

CHAPTER 3
Control on the Track 14

CHAPTER 4
Safety and Speed 22

CHAPTER 5
Racing into the Future 26

Glossary 30
Read More 31
Internet Sites 31
Index 32

IndyCars speed down the track at the 2018 Indy 500 in Indianapolis, Indiana.

CHAPTER 1

THE NEED FOR SPEED

"Drivers, start your engines!" These four words start the famous Indy 500 car race every year. Soon after, specially designed Indy race cars roar down the track in a blur. They reach incredible speeds of more than 200 miles (322 kilometers) per hour. High-tech engines, chassis, and tires rocket these sleek machines past one another as they fight for the win. Hold on to your seats. You're about to go trackside to discover the amazing technology that goes into race cars.

History of Car Racing

Car racing has been around as long as the invention of the automobile. A race in France is widely considered the world's first car race. Forty-six cars raced from Paris to Bordeaux and back in June 1895. The course covered more than 730 miles (1,170 km). Five months later, the first car race in the United States was held in Illinois. Six cars battled it out through mud and snowdrifts in the 54-mile (87-km) *Chicago Times-Herald* race.

FACT

The Indy 500 is called "The Greatest Spectacle in Racing." The first one was held in 1911. In 2018, about 300,000 fans gathered to watch the race.

chassis—the frame on which the body of a vehicle is built

As gas-powered cars gained popularity in the early 1900s, drivers started modifying their cars to make them go faster. Early race cars were often regular production cars. Drivers stripped their cars of doors, roofs, and windshields. Without these parts, the cars were lighter and faster. Some people raced in organized races. But many others raced illegally on streets.

Stock car driver Bill France Sr. leads the pack during a stock car race in 1940.

Over time, different types of car racing started. Organized stock car races began in the 1930s. Drivers used production cars with special seats, tires, and fuel tanks to make them lighter and faster. Stock car drivers raced on oval dirt tracks. At about the same time, drivers in southern California were competing in the first drag races. All of these early racers paved the way for the high-performance vehicles we see today.

FACT

Today the most popular stock car races are in the National Association for Stock Car Auto Racing (NASCAR) series. NASCAR held its first race at Daytona Beach in Florida in 1948.

drag race—a race in which two cars begin at a standstill and drive in a straight line at high speeds for a short distance

modify—to change in some way

production—describes a vehicle produced for mass-market sale

stock car—a car built for racing on oval tracks that is based on the regular model sold to the public

a tube chassis on a Nissan Skyline drag racing car

CHAPTER 2

WHAT MAKES A RACE CAR FAST?

No matter the type, race cars are all built for one thing–speed. For more than 100 years, car designers have been developing new technology to make them faster.

Chassis and Body Design

The car you ride around in every day is likely made of steel. This metal is the most common chassis and body material for street cars. But for many race cars, solid steel is too heavy. Designers use different materials to make race cars as light as possible. Cars racing in NASCAR's Cup Series have bodies made of sheet metal. Sheet metal is much lighter than solid steel. Many drag racing cars use steel tube chassis to reduce weight. Steel tubes are hollow, which makes them light. But they are still very strong.

Formula 1 (F1) cars and IndyCars use carbon fiber in their chassis, cockpit, and outer bodies. Carbon fiber is made of thin strands of carbon. It is both stronger and lighter than steel.

Valtteri Bottas tests his F1 car on the track.

cockpit—the place where the driver sits in a race car

Aerodynamics

Designers build race cars to be aerodynamic so the cars can cut through the air. Air pushes against vehicles as they move, slowing them. The more aerodynamic a car is, the faster it can go. An F1 race car has a narrow, pointed nose that acts like a wedge. It pushes air up and over the car.

Downforce created by the front splitter and spoiler help a NASCAR stock car stay gripped to the track at high speeds.

Race car designers also consider a car's downforce. As air passes over the car, the force of passing air pushes the race car down. This downward force increases the grip of the car's tires on the track. The more grip a car has, the faster it can make turns. FI and IndyCars use rear wings to increase downforce. A NASCAR stock car has a spoiler on its back end. A splitter is also just underneath the front bumper of a NASCAR car. It splits the air hitting it, creating downforce for the front of the car.

PUTTING THE BODY TO THE TEST

FI designers run tests in wind tunnels to see how air flows over smaller models of their cars. Powerful fans blow air over, under, and through a car's body. Designers make changes to their cars based on the results. FI rules limit the time teams can spend doing tests in wind tunnels. These rules help keep one team from having an advantage over another.

Workers get a Sauber FI car ready for wind tunnel tests.

aerodynamic—built to move easily through the air

spoiler—a wing-shaped part attached to a sports car that helps improve the car's handling

a turbocharger attached to an engine

FACT
Some production cars come with superchargers. The 2019 Camaro has a supercharged V-8 engine. It can reach 60 miles (97 km) per hour in 3.5 seconds.

Engines

The engine is the heart of a race car. Like other parts, designers build and modify them to meet the needs of each race car. For example, drag racing car engines are built to accelerate very quickly. NASCAR engines are designed to run at top speed for hundreds of miles.

A NASCAR engine sits in the inspection area during race practice.

In early stock car racing, racers used the same engines that came in the production models. Today NASCAR engines are made specially for racing. They are much larger than standard car engines.

The more air that rushes into an engine, the faster it can go. Some race cars use superchargers to increase air flow to the engine. As the engine runs, it powers the supercharger. The supercharger then pumps air into the engine. Other race cars, such as F1 and IndyCars, use turbochargers. Turbochargers are similar to superchargers. But they use the car's exhaust gases to bring air into the engine.

accelerate—to increase the speed of a moving object

exhaust gas—the waste gas produced by a car

PIt stop crew members rush to change the tires on Joey Logano's NASCAR car in a 2018 race.

CHAPTER 3

CONTROL ON THE TRACK

Engines roar as two drag race cars sit side-by-side at the starting line. Yellow lights flash on the light post between them. Then the green light comes on—go! Now it's up to the drivers to control the race cars at incredible speeds. This is where more tech comes into play. Control is a big part of racing.

Tires

With one slip of a tire, a race car can run off course or crash. Drag racing, F1, IndyCar, and NASCAR cars use smooth tires called slicks. These smooth tires create a great deal of friction with the paved track. A paved track is covered with asphalt or another material that makes the track hard. On these surfaces, smooth tires provide good grip.

Slicks often need to be changed several times during a race. Friction between the tires and the track makes a lot of heat. A hot tire does not work as well. It also wears down quickly.

Race cars have tires with tread for unpaved surfaces. Rally cars race off road. The tires need tread to help them grip loose surfaces, such as dirt and sand. Tread also helps push water away. IndyCars and other race cars sometimes use tires with tread in rain.

friction— a force created when two objects rub together

tread—a series of bumps and deep grooves on a tire

Nitrogen-Filled Tires

Unlike regular car tires, NASCAR stock car tires are filled with nitrogen. As a car races along, the tires get very hot. Excess moisture in the air heats up and expands, increasing tire pressure. This increased pressure can reduce handling or cause a blow-out. Nitrogen has less moisture than regular air. It keeps tire pressure down.

FACT

Car company McLaren invented the inerter used in F1 cars. They came up with the name "J-damper" to keep it a secret from other teams.

Off-road vehicles need to have strong suspension systems to handle jumps.

Suspension Systems

In car racing, contact with the road means more control and more speed. Designers have created different suspension designs for different racing conditions. On paved, level courses, a stiff suspension increases the vehicle's contact with the road. F1 cars use inerters to absorb excess vibration from the tires and keep the cars even more stable.

Off-road racers speed over rough land. They go right over large bumps and fly through the air. For these brave racers, a stiff suspension would mean lots of rough landings! Rally cars have big shocks to handle these extreme conditions. Large shocks heat up quickly. As shocks heat up, they don't work as well. Some off-road racers use an external cooling system called a "cactus cooler." It can reduce the temperature of a shock's fluid by 100 degrees Fahrenheit (38 degrees Celsius).

nitrogen—a colorless, odorless gas suspension—the system of springs and shock absorbers that absorbs a car's up-and-down movements

The hot brakes of an Audi R8 glow as it speeds down a racetrack.

Brakes

The brakes used in most street cars are called disc brakes. They are usually made of cast iron. For modern race cars, cast iron brakes are too heavy. They also don't last long under extreme speeds. Some race cars use lighter and more durable brake materials, such as ceramic. Ceramic material can withstand hotter temperatures involved in braking. F1 and IndyCars use carbon brakes. Carbon is even lighter and stronger than ceramic.

When a driver steps on the brake pedal, the brake pads pinch the rotors attached to the wheels. This contact creates friction to stop the car. But it also creates heat. The hottest most street car brakes will ever get is 400°F (204°C). Race car brakes reach temperatures of more than 1,000°F (538°C). In some races, so much heat is produced from braking that you can actually see the brakes glowing red. If brakes get too hot, they don't work as well. Many race teams monitor brake heat using temperature-sensitive paint. As the paint heats up, its color changes. To keep brakes cool, some race cars have air ducts that take air in from the front of the car and move it to the brakes.

a carbon brake

Turning and Handling

The ability to turn corners while maintaining high speed can mean the difference between winning and losing a race. Centripetal force is what makes a race car change direction when a driver steers around a turn. It takes more than 10,000 pounds (4,536 kilograms) of centripetal force to turn a NASCAR stock car around a corner at 180 miles (290 km) per hour. This puts a lot of pressure on the steering system. NASCAR and other race cars have strong steering wheels. Some steering wheels are made of aluminium or carbon fiber. These materials are both strong and lightweight.

A NASCAR steering wheel has a leather covering to improve grip for the driver.

The steering wheel in most race cars also has a very small turning radius. The turning radius is how much a driver has to turn the steering wheel to turn the wheels. In a regular street car, drivers can turn the steering wheel a couple of times. In race cars, a small turn of the steering wheel allows drivers to take sharp corners at high speeds.

FIGHTING SIDEFORCE

Sharp turns at high speeds create sideforce. This force pushes the car sideways during a turn. To control this, designers have added end plates to the rear wing of many racing cars. The end plates push back on the sideforce to keep the car from going into a spin.

centripetal force—the force that pulls an object turning in a circle inward toward the center

A roll cage is made of bars surrounding the cockpit.

CHAPTER 4

SAFETY AND SPEED

Car racing and danger go hand in hand. Drivers risk serious injury or even death when they get behind the wheel. Safety tech lessens these risks.

Inside the Cockpit

Roll cages are standard safety equipment for race cars. A roll cage is made of extra-thick metal tubing. It surrounds the driver and provides protection in case of a rollover.

FI and IndyCars have open cockpits. These cars use roll bars or hoops that stick up from the car for protection during rollovers. In 2018, FI cars added the Halo. This hoop is designed to protect drivers from flying objects.

NASCAR ROOF FLAPS

Special flaps are built into the roofs of NASCAR cars. During a crash, a car often spins out of control. The flaps help keep the car from flipping by changing the air flow over the car. They keep the car from lifting.

The safety belt in most race cars is a tight-fitting five-point harness. It is made from strong material such as nylon. Two straps come down over the driver's shoulders, two straps go across the waist, and one comes up between the legs. Safety harnesses in F1 cars can have up to seven points.

The Driver's Equipment

It's not just the car's safety tech that can protect a driver. Drivers also depend on their clothing and gear.

Fires can happen in all types of car racing. Drivers wear fire-resistant suits. These suits are made of two to four layers of fire-resistant material. Air pockets between each layer reduce heat transfer, further protecting the driver. Fire-resistant material may also be woven into the cloth that makes up a driver's gloves, socks, shoes, and helmet lining.

FACT

A NASCAR car has a window net on the left side instead of a window. It keeps the driver's arms from flying out of the window during a crash.

Helmets protect a driver's head in a crash. Most helmets have an outer shell made of a special layer of resin. This resin is a combination of carbon fiber and other materials. Underneath this shell, a special foam layer absorbs the energy caused by a hit to the head.

Kevin Harvick sits in the cockpit of his NASCAR car fully dressed in his safety gear.

Formula E car bodies are made of carbon fiber and another strong material called Kevlar.

CHAPTER 5

RACING INTO THE FUTURE

Race car designers are constantly coming up with new technologies to improve performance and safety. Some companies focus on creating stronger materials for car bodies. These materials can help keep a car's body together during a crash. With fewer parts scattered on the track, other drivers are safer.

FACT

Unlike a regular F1 car, a Formula E's wheels are enclosed in the body. It also has a V-shaped rear wing. Both design changes cut down on drag.

Some designers are experimenting with electric race cars. An electric Formula E car looks much like a regular F1 car. But the engine relies on an electric battery for power instead of gasoline. Previous Formula E batteries lasted just half the race. Designers have improved the battery so it lasts the whole race. Companies continue to improve batteries for future Formula E cars.

Concept Cars

The future of race cars seems limited only by the imagination of car designers. Concept cars are designed to show ideas. Only some of them go into production for people to buy.

The Renault FI 2027 concept car looks like it came straight out of a science-fiction movie. The hybrid car has both a gas-powered engine and an electric engine. It has four-wheel drive to improve handling. Two roll bars automatically rise out of the cockpit to keep the driver safe during a rollover.

FACT

The Roborace company designed a completely self-driving race car called the Robocar. It is the world's first driverless electric race car.

The McLaren Senna GTR appeared at the International Motor Show in Switzerland in 2018.

Unlike current FI cars, the Renault FI 2027 has a covered cockpit.

The McLaren Senna GTR concept car pushes the limits of sports car racing. In this type of racing, the cars are designed to compete over long distances. The McLaren Senna GTR has a large splitter under the front bumper. The sides of the car are pushed in to allow better air flow. The car's wing has a Gurney flap. It helps suck hot air away from the engine.

Technology continues to push race cars to faster speeds with better control and safety. The future could bring more electric cars and even self-driving cars to the racing world. As the tech advances, pulse-pounding thrills are sure to follow for both drivers and fans.

GLOSSARY

accelerate (ak-SEL-uh-rayt)—to increase the speed of a moving object

aerodynamic (air-oh-dye-NA-mik)—built to move easily through the air

centripetal force (sen-TRI-puh-tuhl FORS)—the force that pulls an object turning in a circle inward toward the center

chassis (CHA-see)—the frame on which the body of a vehicle is built

cockpit (KOK-pit)—the place where the driver sits in a race car

drag race (DRAG RAYS)—a race in which two cars begin at a standstill and drive in a straight line at high speeds for a short distance

exhaust gas (ig-ZAWST GAS)—the waste gas produced by a car

friction (FRIK-shuhn)—a force created when two objects rub together

modify (MAH-duh-fye)—to change in some way

nitrogen (NYE-truh-juhn)—a colorless, odorless gas

production (pruh-DUHK-shuhn)—describes a vehicle produced for mass-market sale

spoiler (SPOIL-uhr)—a wing-shaped part attached to a sports car that helps improve the car's handling

stock car (STOK CAR)—a car built for racing on oval tracks that is based on the regular model sold to the public

suspension (suh-SPEN-shuhn)—the system of springs and shock absorbers that absorbs a car's up-and-down movements

tread (TRED)—a series of bumps and deep grooves on a tire

READ MORE

Brooklyn, Billie. *Sports Car Racing.* Checkered Flag. New York: PowerKids Press, 2015.

Gray, Leon. *Fast and Cool Cars.* DK Adventures. New York: DK, Penguin Random House, 2015.

Weber, M. *Wild Moments of Stock Car Racing.* Wild Moments of Motorsports. North Mankato, MN: Capstone Press, 2017.

INTERNET SITES

Anatomy of an IndyCar
https://www.indycar.com/Fan-Info/INDYCAR-101/The-Car-Dallara/Anatomy-Of-An-INDYCAR

Science of Speed: Turning
https://www.nsf.gov/news/special_reports/sos/turning.jsp

Understanding F1 Racing
https://www.formula1.com/en/championship/inside-f1/understanding-f1-racing.html

INDEX

brakes, 18–19

"cactus coolers," 17
carbon fiber, 9, 20, 25
chassis, 4, 9
Chicago Times-Herald race, 5
cockpits, 9, 23
concept cars, 27, 28, 29

downforce, 11
drag racing cars, 7, 9, 12, 14, 15

end plates, 21
engines, 4, 12–13, 14, 27, 28, 29

fire-resistant suits, 24
Formula 1 (F1) cars, 9, 10, 11, 13, 15, 16, 17, 18, 23, 24, 27, 28
Formula E cars, 27

Gurney flaps, 29

Halo, 23
helmets, 24, 25

Indy 500, 4, 5
Indy race cars, 4, 9, 11, 13, 15, 18, 23
inerters, 16, 17

nitrogen, 16

off-road race cars, 15, 17

rally cars, 15
roll bars, 23, 28
roll cages, 23

safety harnesses, 24
shocks, 17
slicks, 15
splitters, 11, 29
spoilers, 11
steering wheels, 20–21
stock cars, 7, 13
    NASCAR race cars, 7, 9, 11, 12, 13, 15, 16, 20, 23, 24
superchargers, 13
suspension systems, 17

turbochargers, 13

wind tunnels, 11